HISTORY

OF THE

WAR IN SOUTH AFRICA

1899–1902

COMPILED BY DIRECTION OF
HIS MAJESTY'S GOVERNMENT

BY

MAJOR-GENERAL SIR FREDERICK MAURICE, K.C.B.

WITH A STAFF OF OFFICERS

MAPS • VOLUME IV

The Naval & Military Press Ltd

Published by
The Naval & Military Press Ltd
5 Riverside, Brambleside, Bellbrook
Industrial Estate, Uckfield, East Sussex,
TN22 1QQ England
Tel: +44 (0) 1825 749494
Fax: +44 (0) 1825 765701
www.naval-military-press.com

*In reprinting in facsimile from the original, any imperfections are inevitably reproduced
and the quality may fall short of modern type and cartographic standards.*

LIST OF MAPS.
VOL. IV.

MAPS

No. 56. EASTERN TRANSVAAL.

No. 57. THE ACTION AT BAKENLAAGTE. October 30th, 1901.

No. 58. SOUTH AFRICA. May, 1902. *Map showing line of Blockhouses, Stationary Garrisons and Posts.*

No. 59. WESTERN TRANSVAAL.

No. 60. GEN. SIR IAN HAMILTON'S "DRIVE" IN THE WESTERN TRANSVAAL. May 6th to 11th, 1902.

No. 61. PLAN OF RAILWAY LINE. *Illustrating system of Blockhouses, etc., generally adopted.*

No. 62. PLAN OF ROAD BETWEEN MACHADODORP AND LYDENBURG. *Illustrating system of Blockhouses, etc., generally adopted.*

No. 63. CAPE COLONY.

No. 64. ORANGE RIVER COLONY.

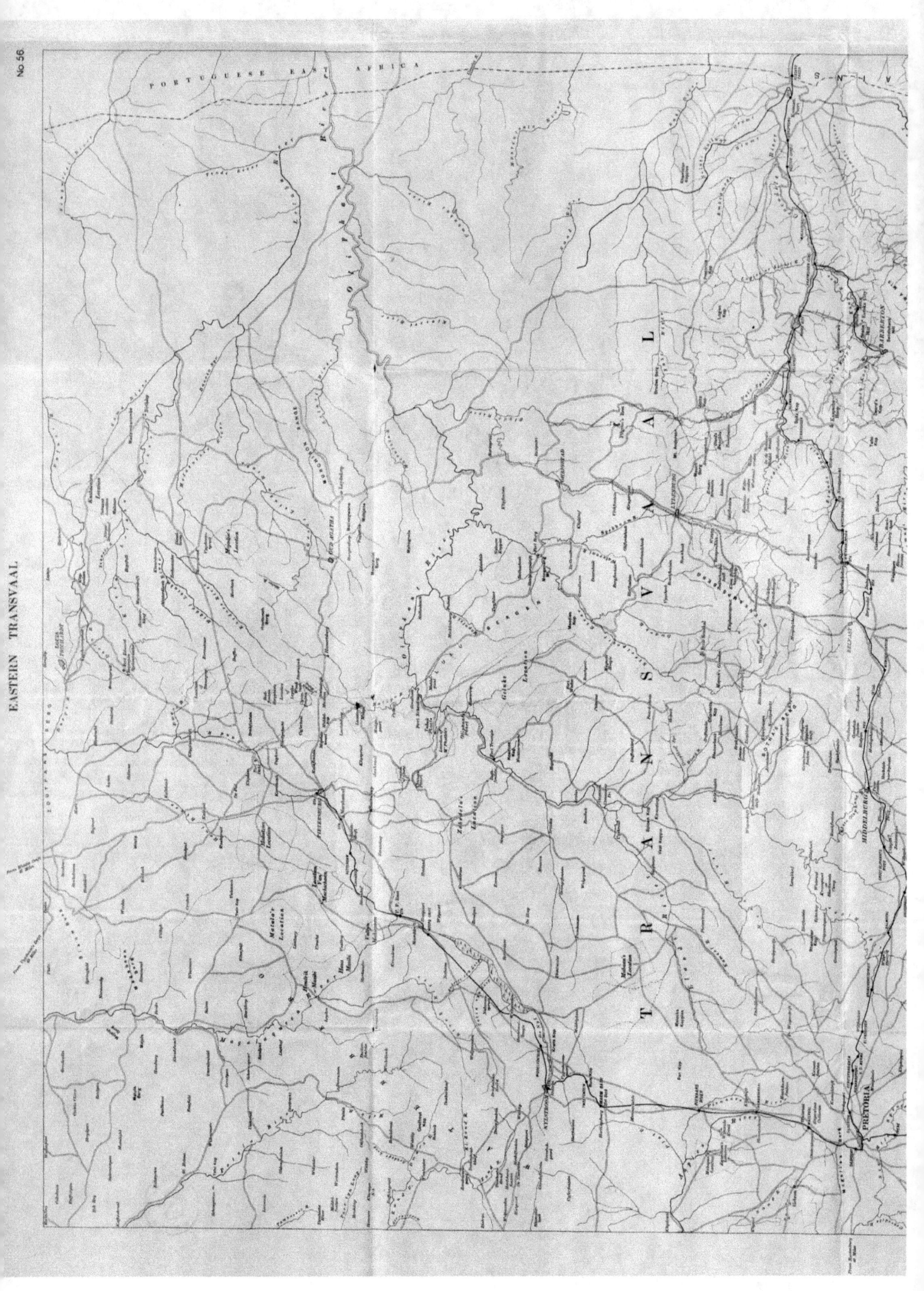

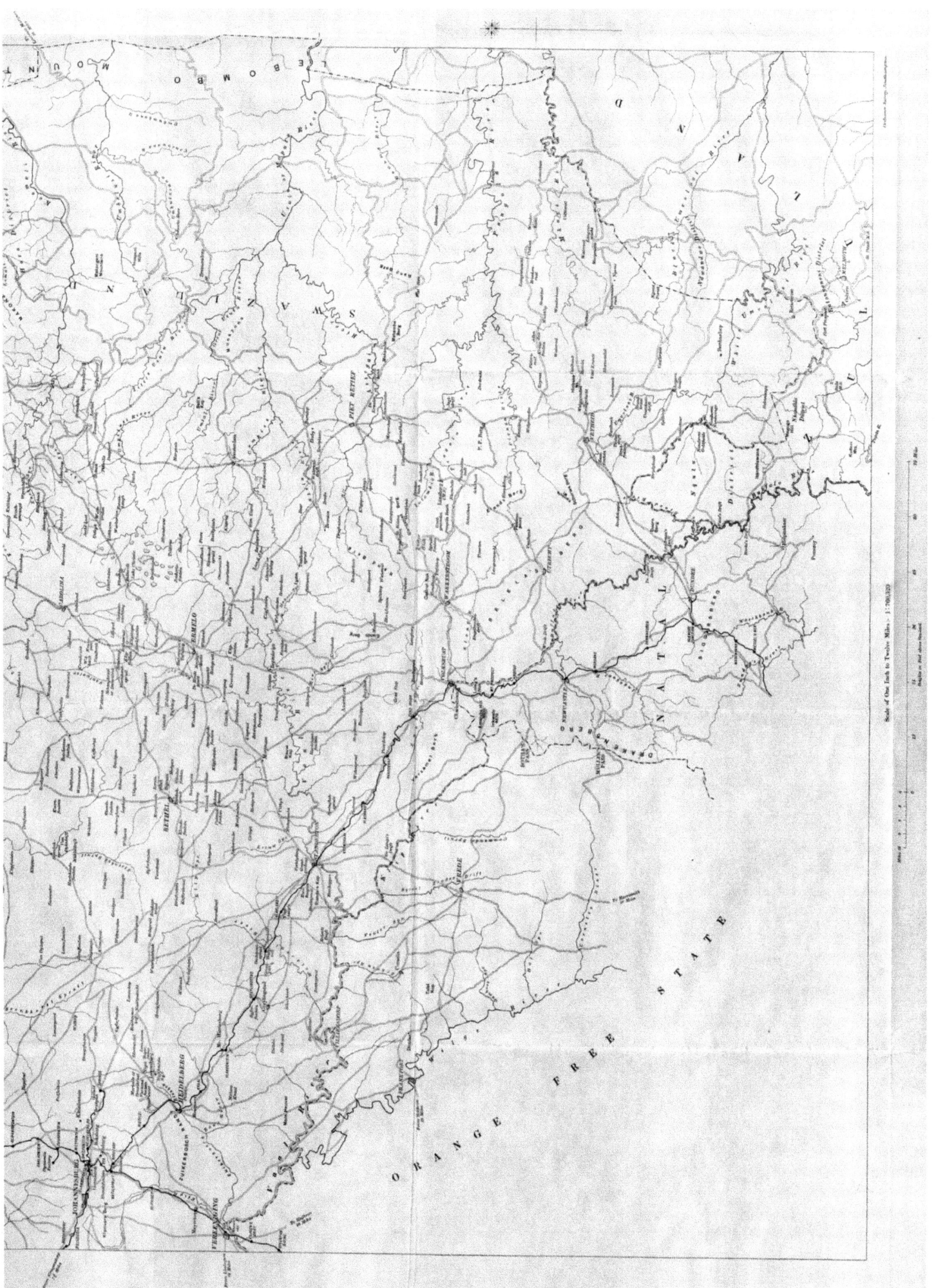

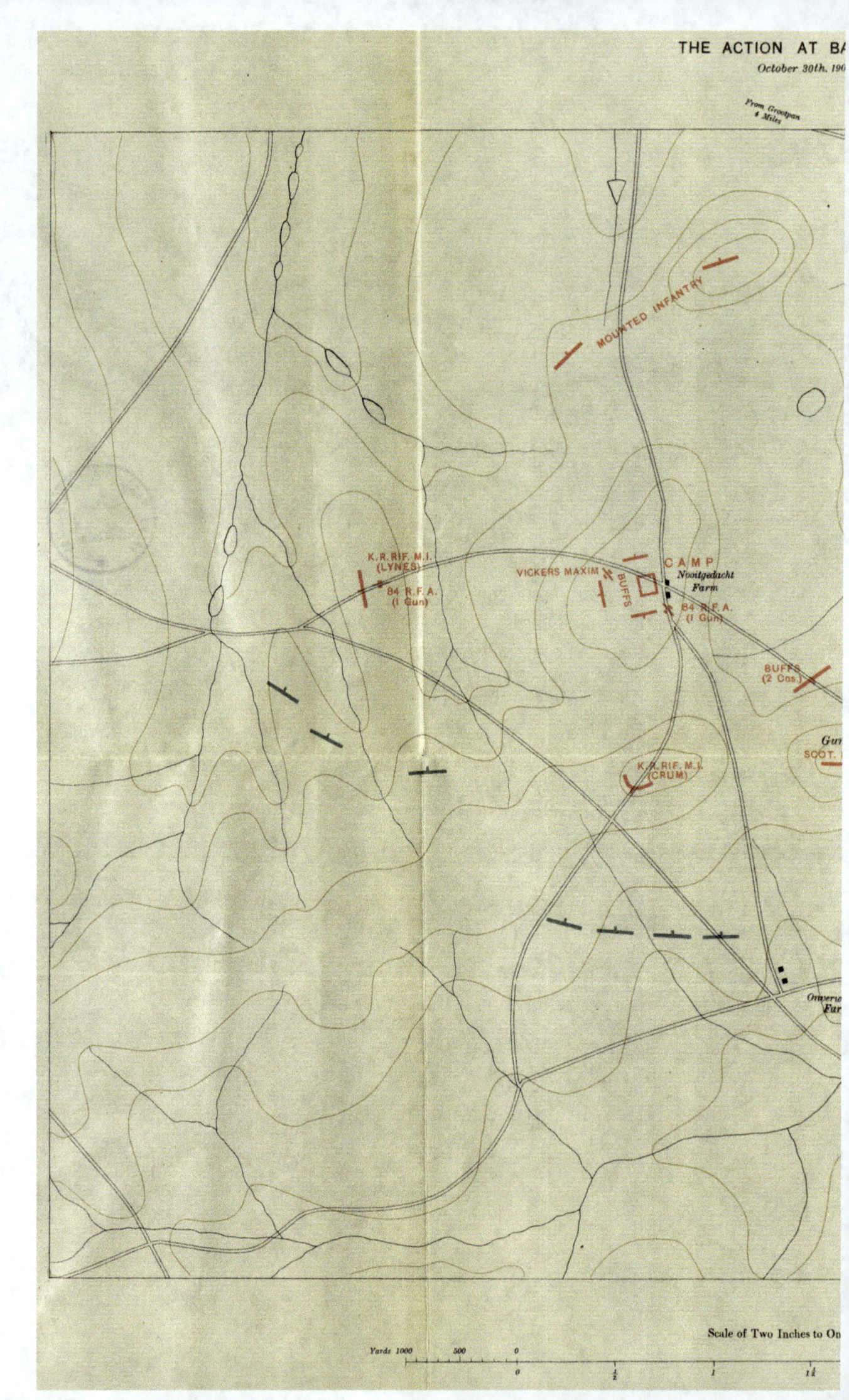

THE ACTION AT BA[KENLAAGTE]
October 30th, 190[2]

Scale of Two Inches to On[e Mile]

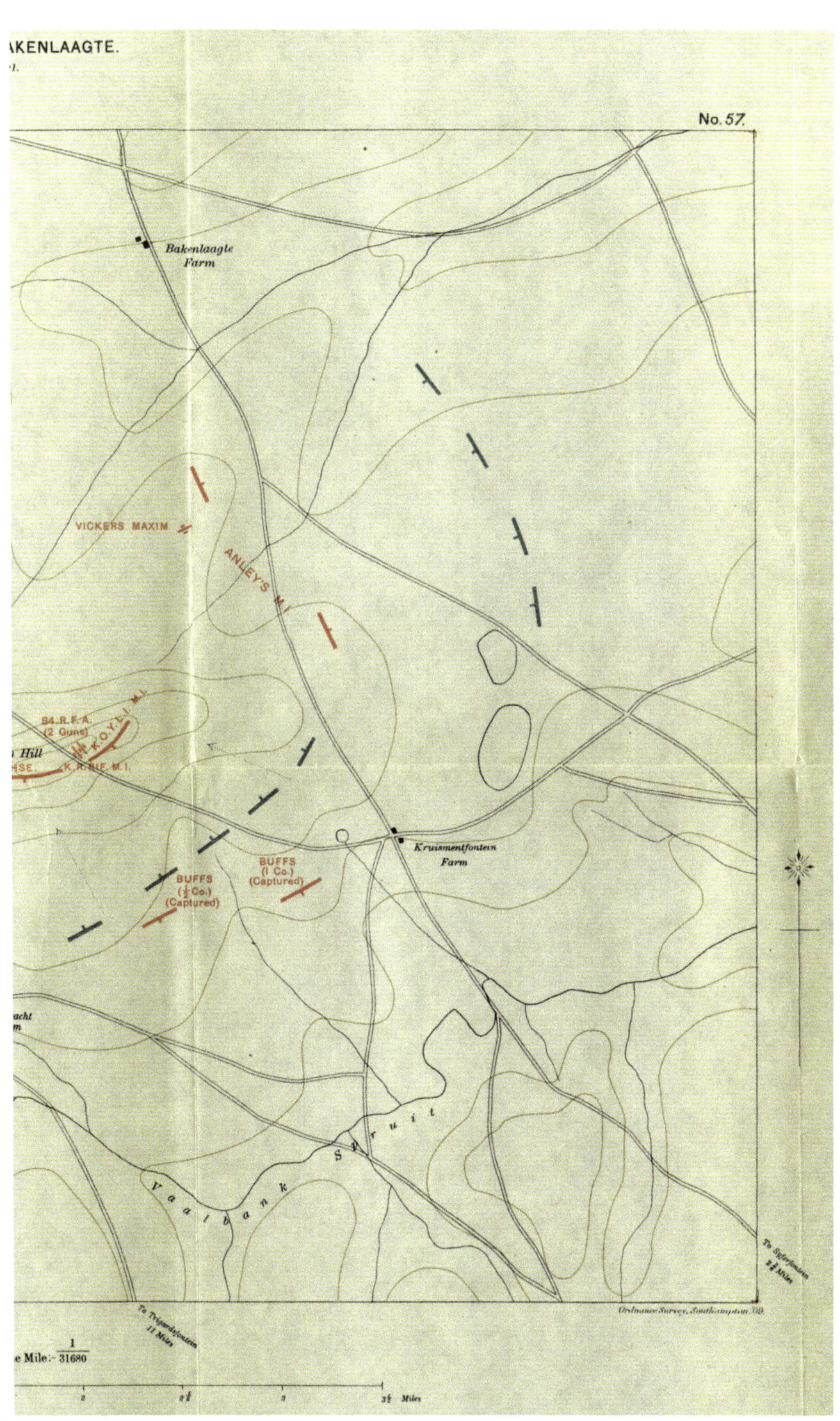

SOUTH
Map showing line of Blockhouses

AFRICA.
Stationary Garrisons & Posts.

No. 58.

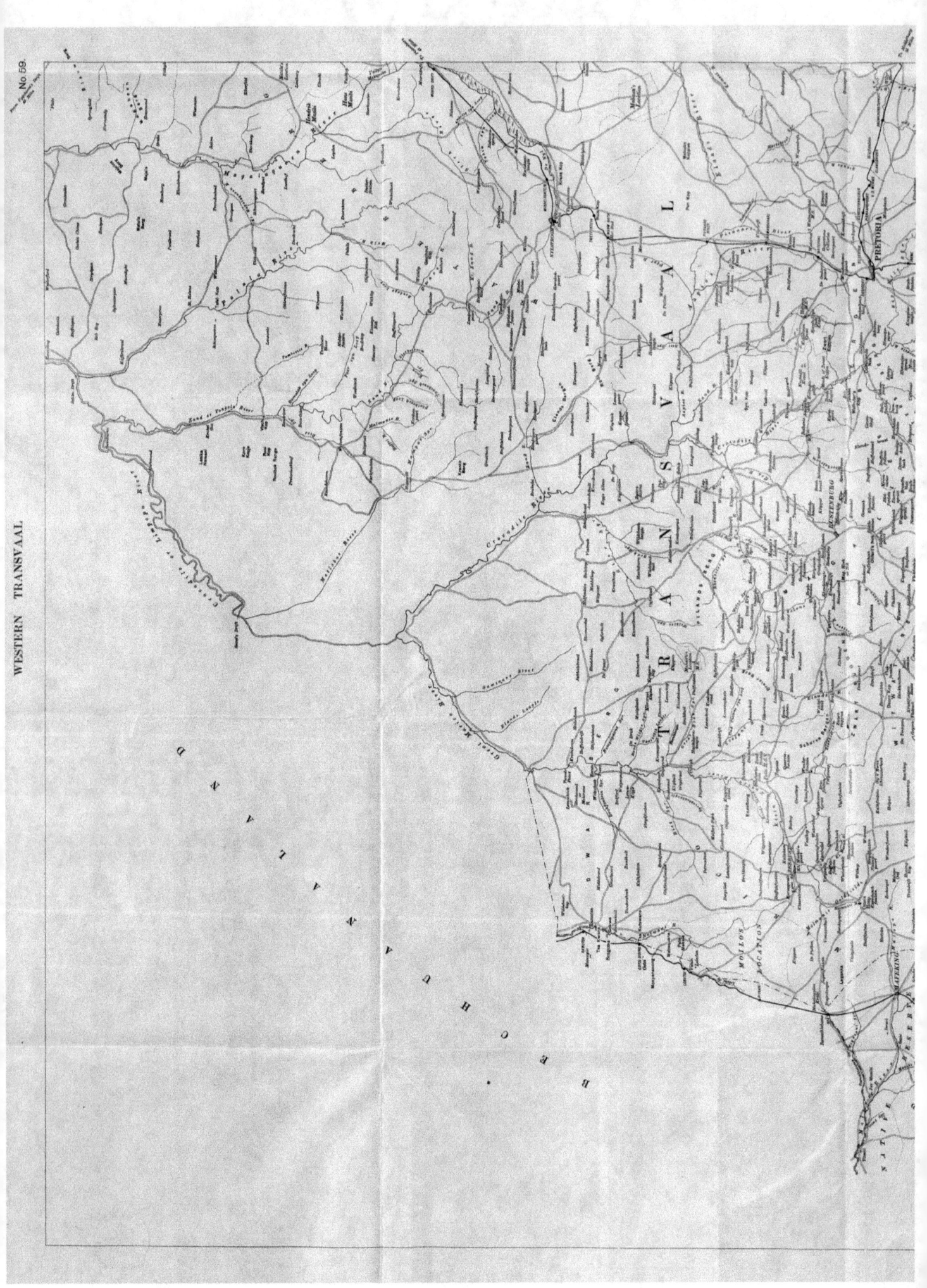

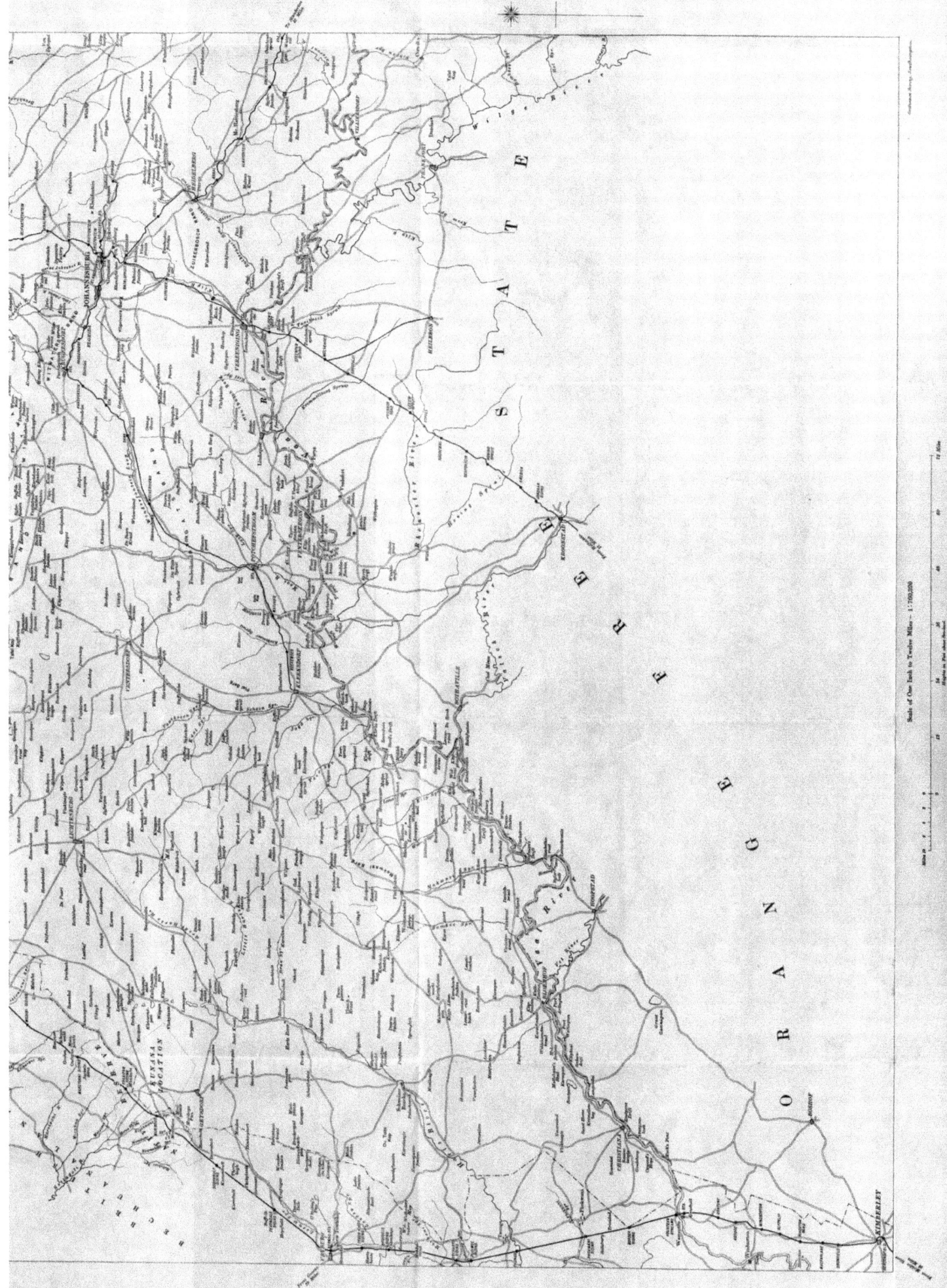

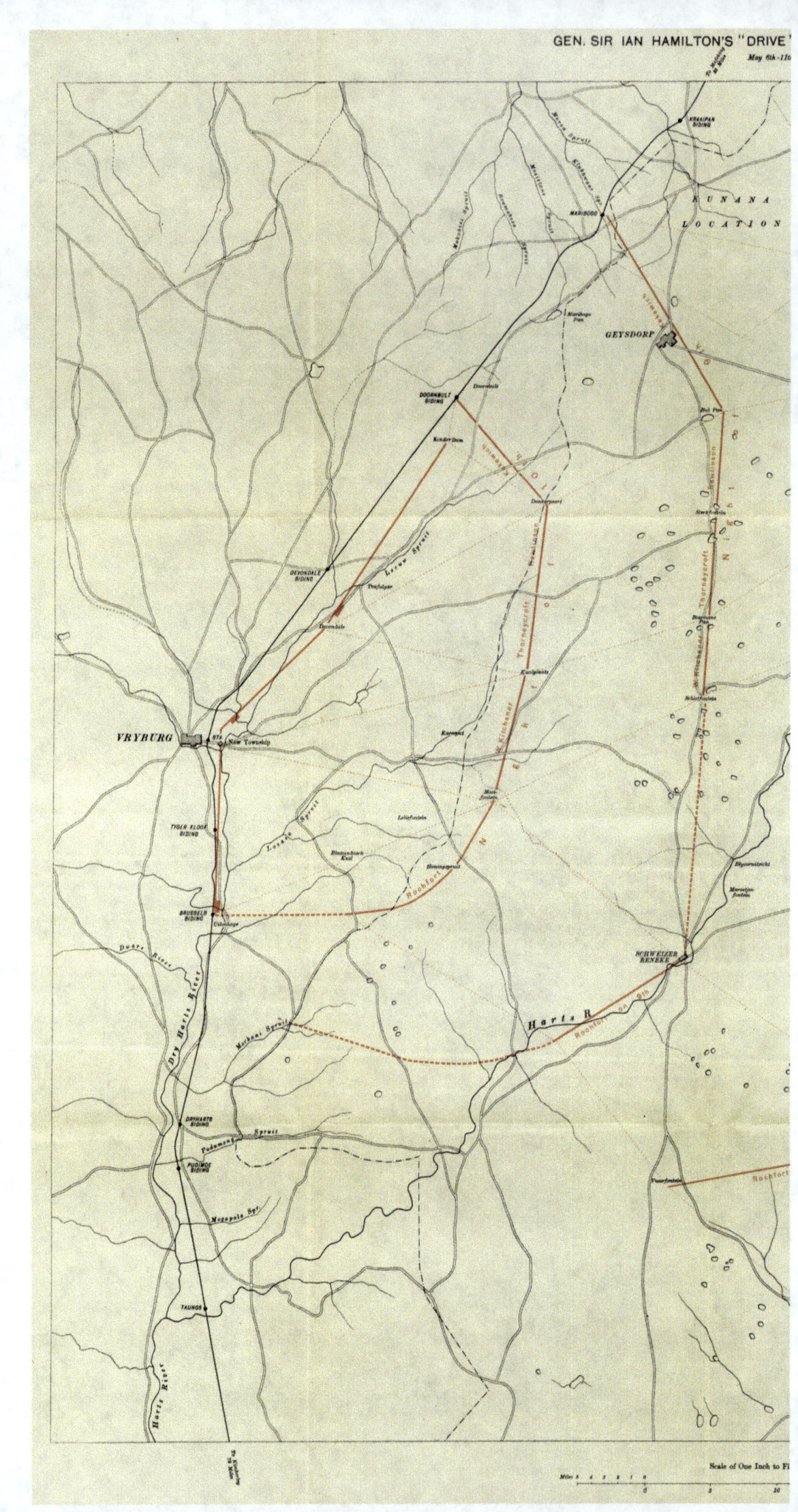

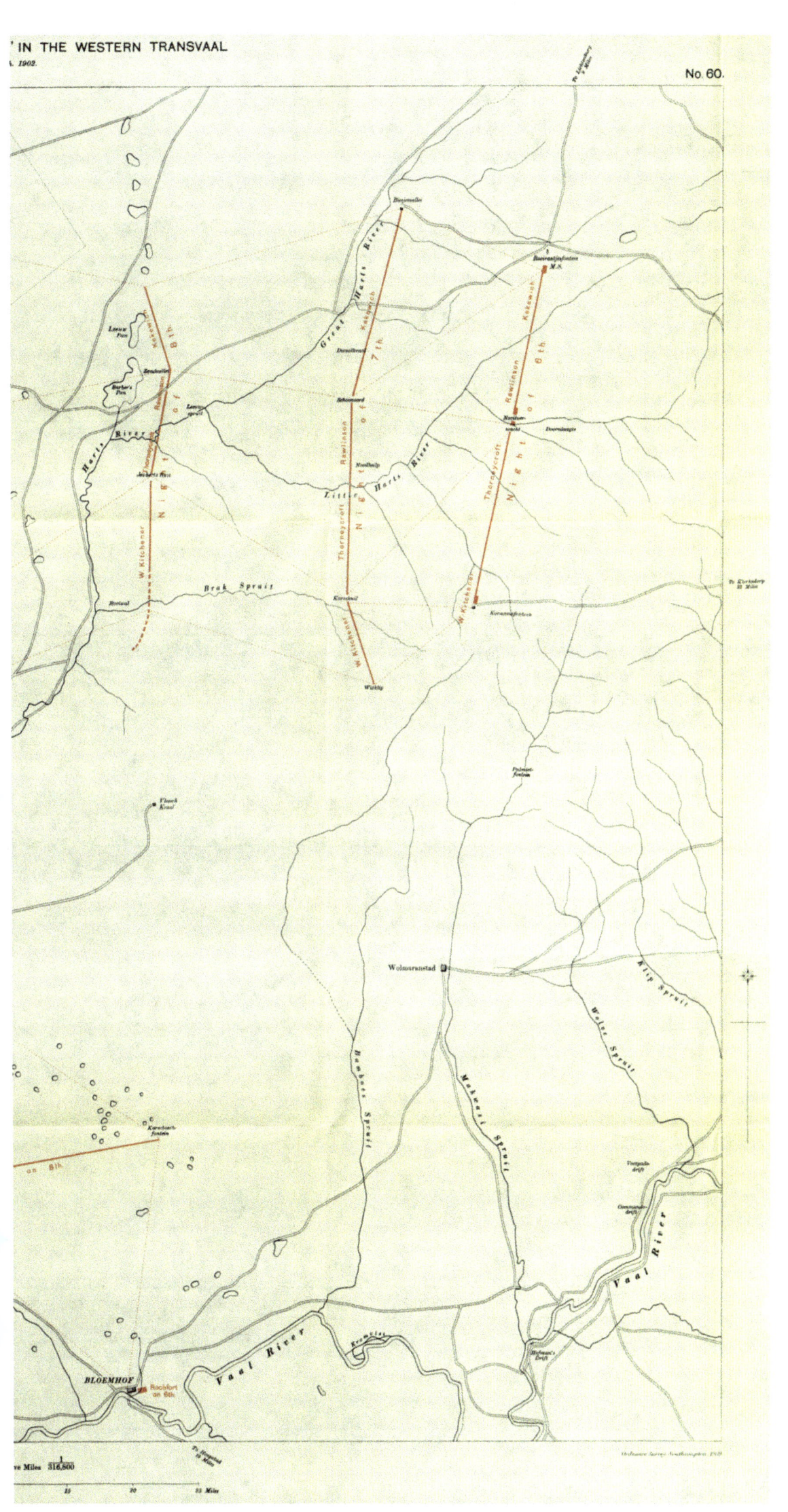

REFERENCE

Circular Blockhouses	●
,, ,, kneeling	●
Octagonal ,,	⬢
Rectangular & Square Blockhouses	▬ ■
Masonry Blockhouses	⊗
Bridge	▬
Ganger's Huts defended	▭
Loose Stone Blockhouses with Shields	⌣
,, ,, ,, without ,,	⌣
Closed Earthworks	⌒
,, Sangar work	▽
Alarm Guns	⅄
Wire on Standards	++++++++
,, Criss Cross	✕✕✕✕✕
,, I.M.R. Electrical	⊙⊙⊙⊙⊙
Railway Trench deepened & improved	───

Wildfontein — 284, 280, 275

BELFAST — 260, 255

236, 235, 230

WATERVAL BOVEN — North Hill, West B. House, East B. House, Ridge Posts, 212, 210, 205, Tunnel, Natives, Camp Post, Reserves, Bluff B. House, Examining Guard, South Hill

WATERVAL ONDER

NOOITGEDACHT — 188, 185, 180

ELANDSHOEK — 164, 160, 155, Level Crossing

Mile 1   ¾   ½   ¼   0

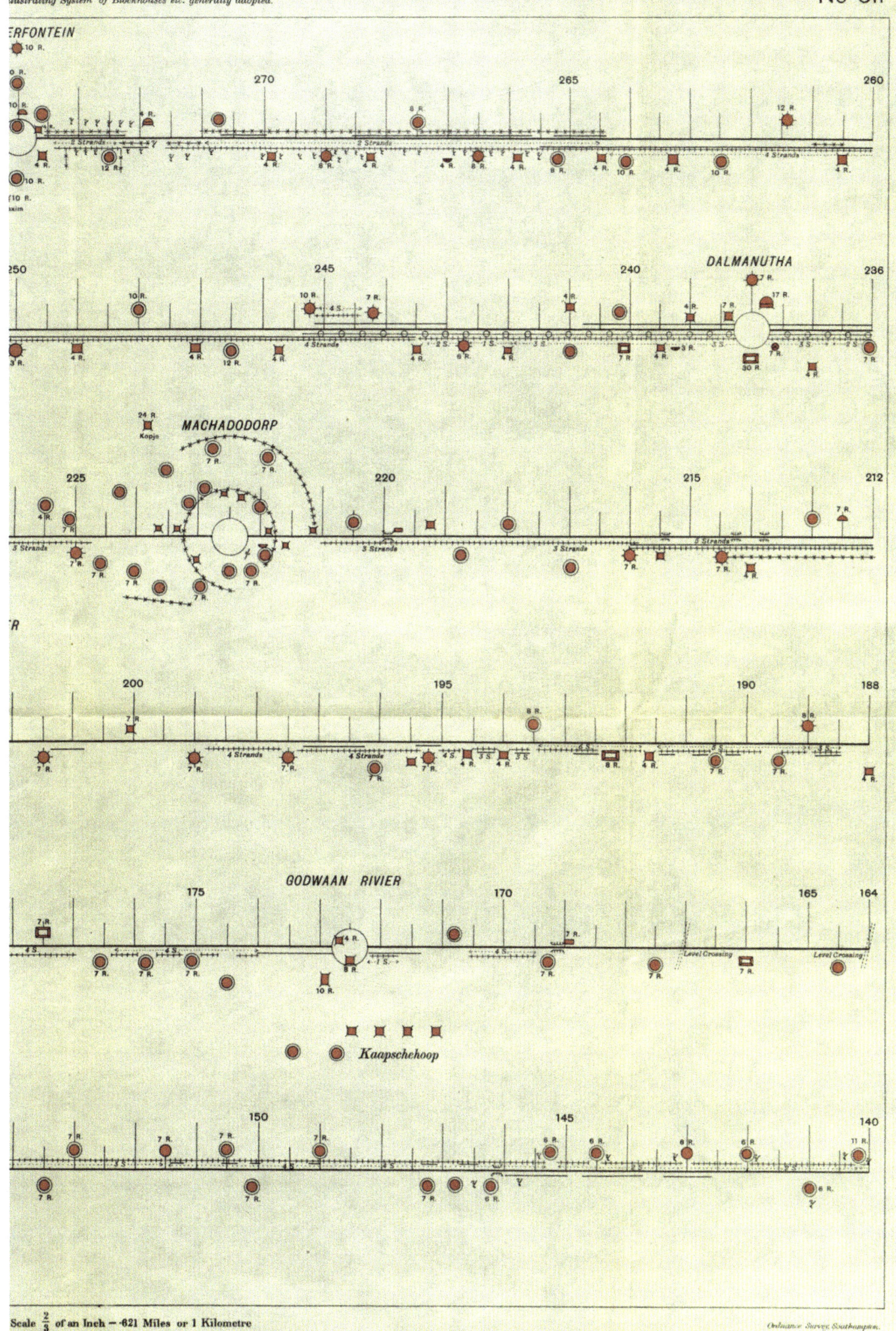

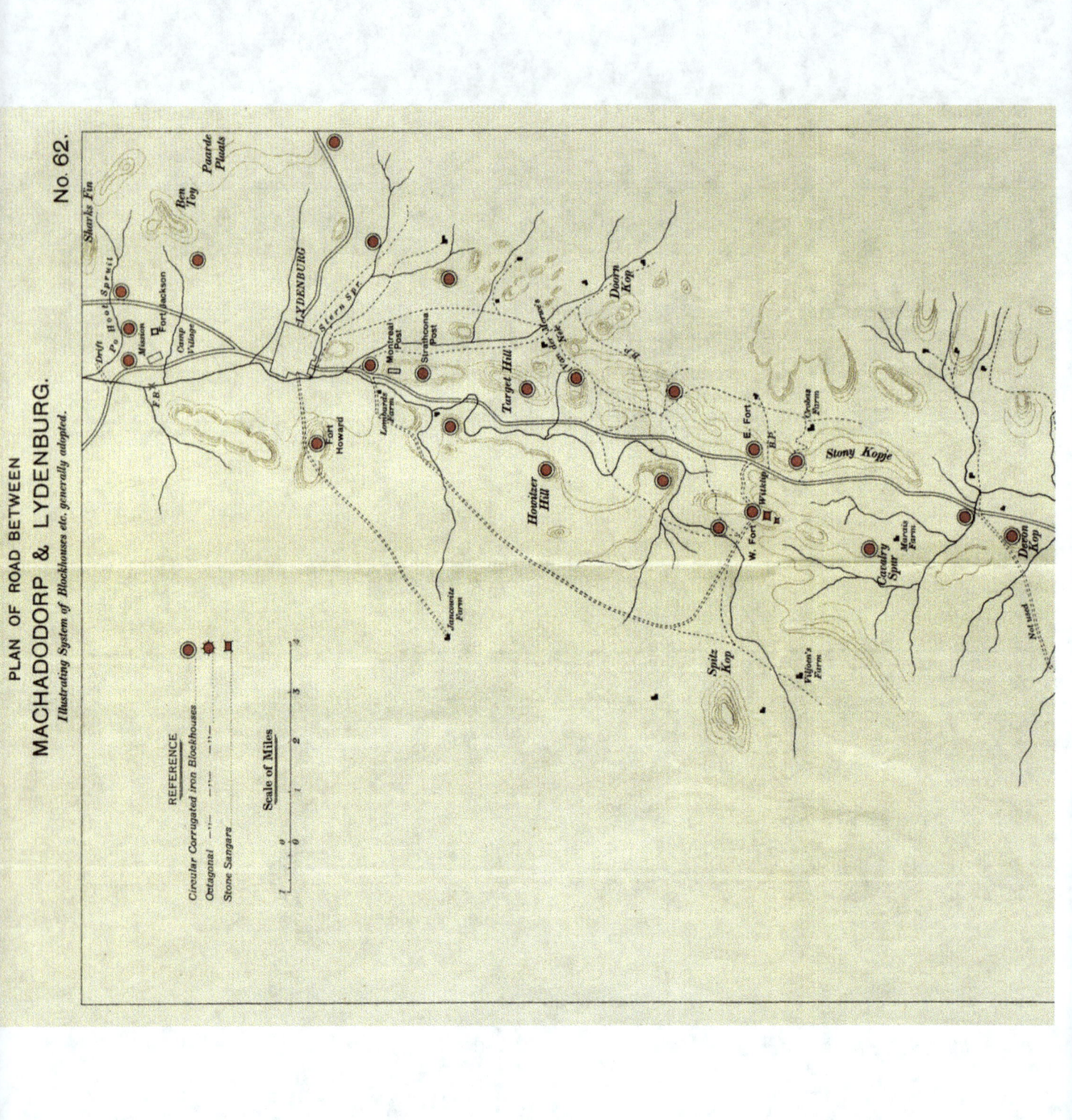

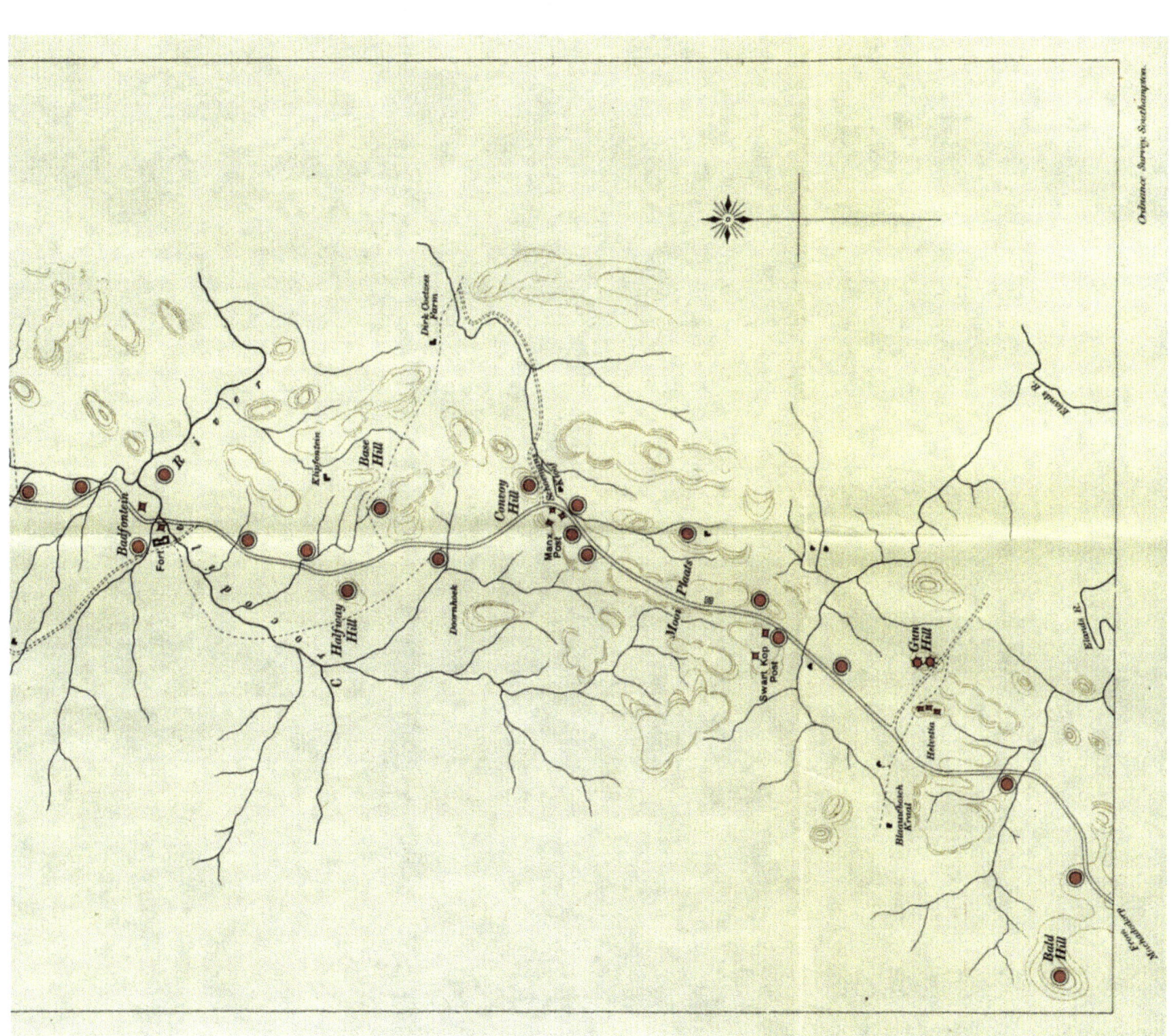

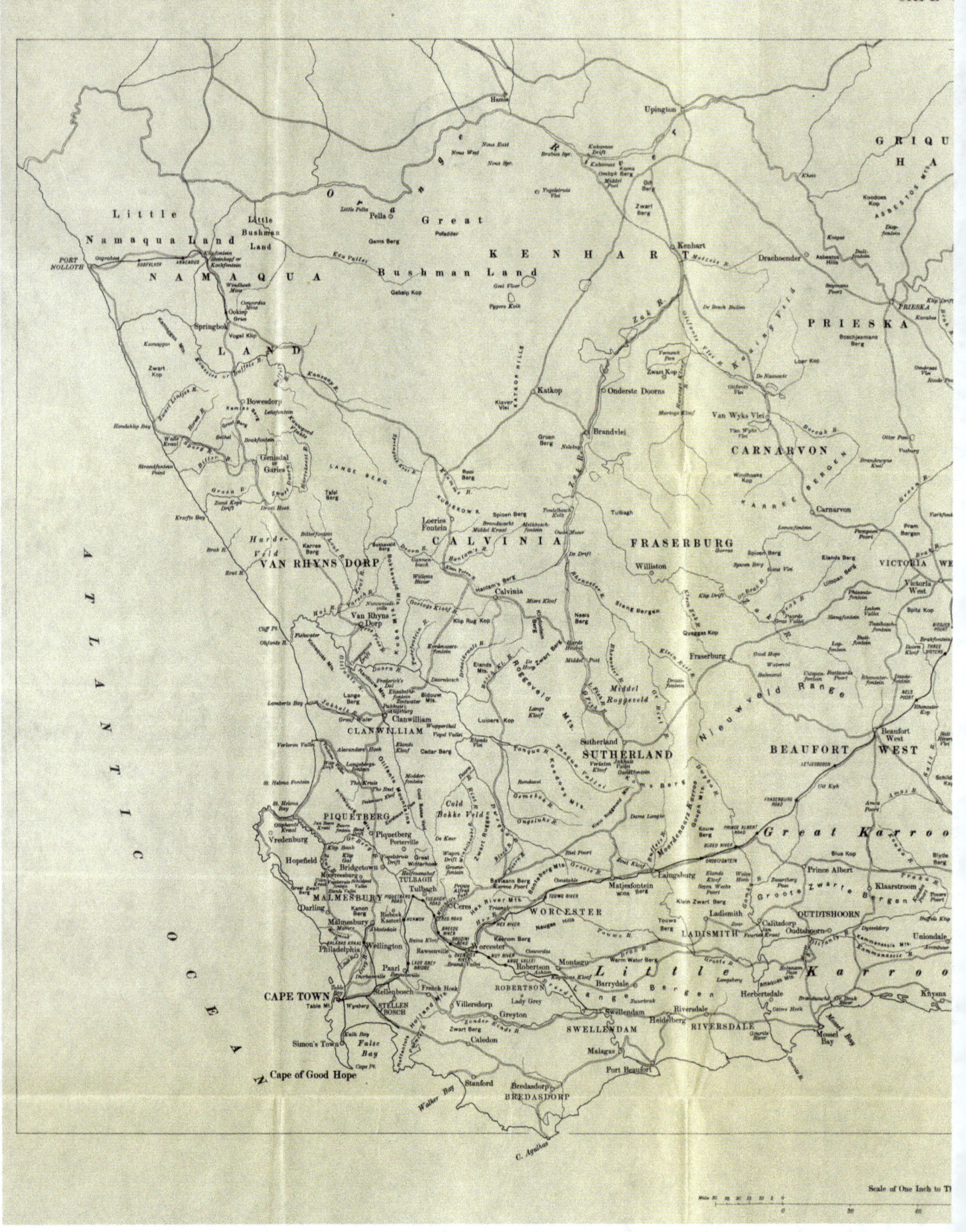

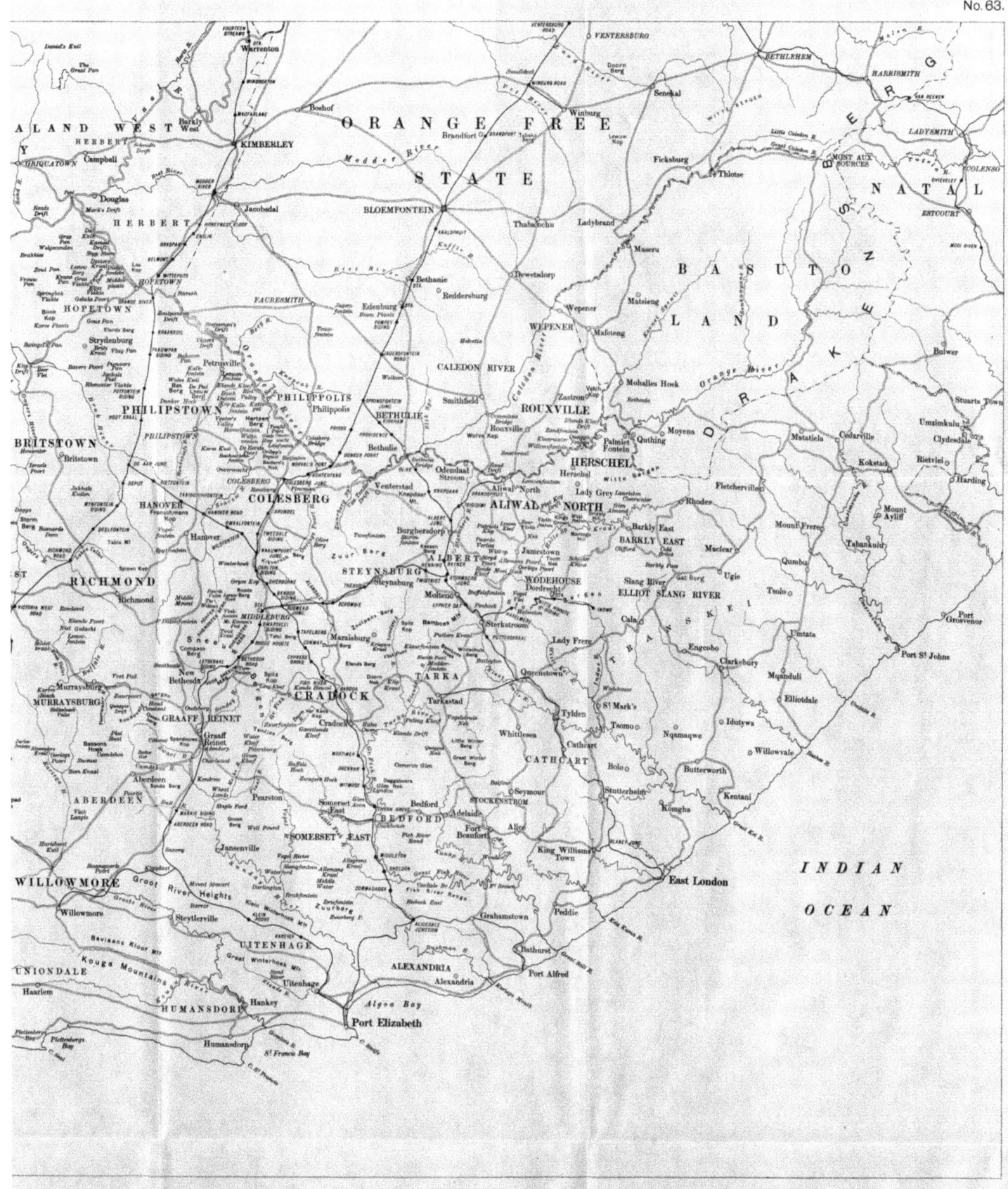

No. 63.

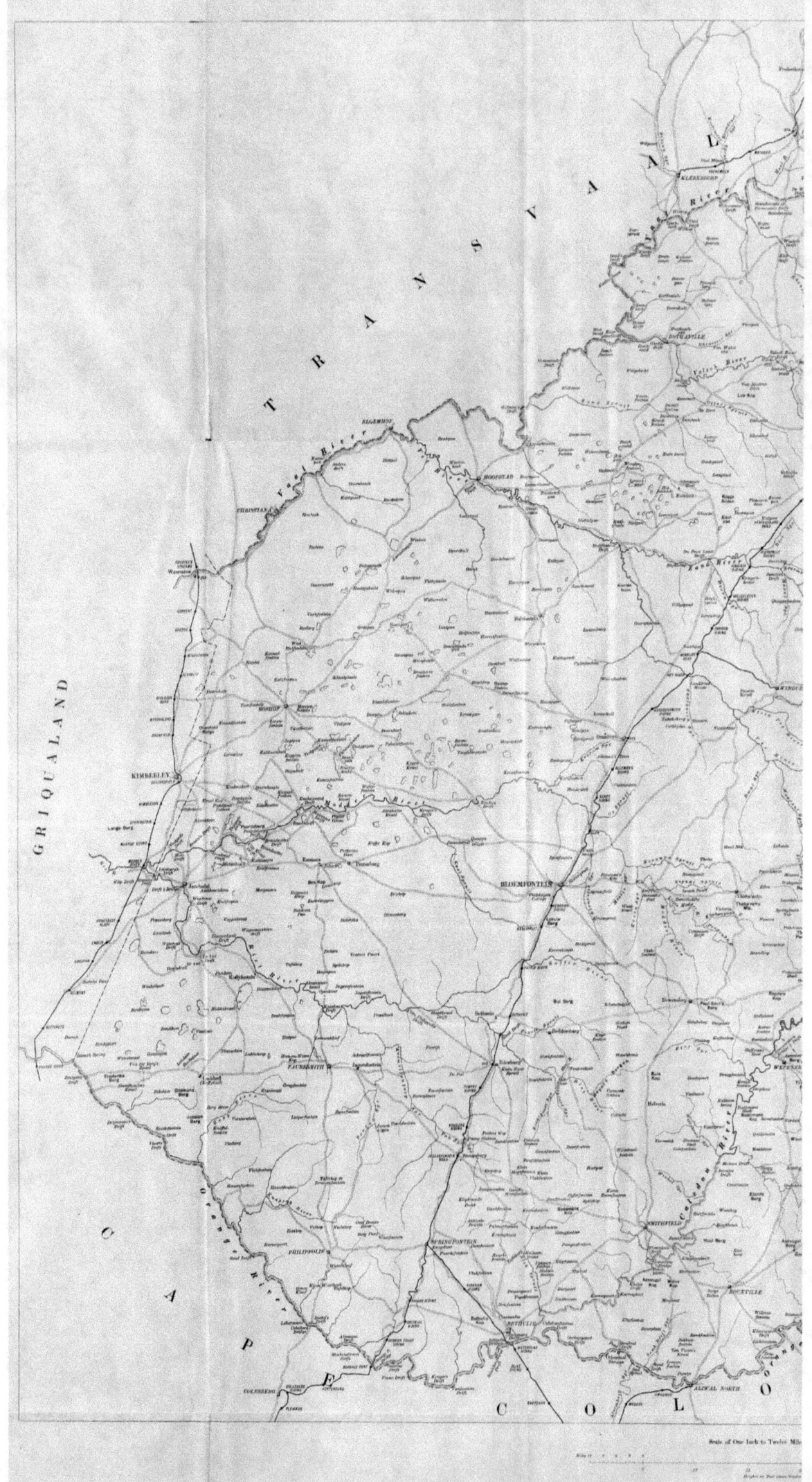

No. 64.

Notes

Notes

Notes

Notes

Notes

Notes

Notes

Notes

Notes

Notes

Notes

Notes

Notes

Notes

Notes

Notes

Notes

Notes

Notes

Notes

Notes

www.ingramcontent.com/pod-product-compliance
Lightning Source LLC
Chambersburg PA
CBHW080834010526
44112CB00016B/2515